Our Muscles

Susan Thames

Rourke
Publishing LLC
Vero Beach, Florida 32964

www.rourkepublishing.com

PHOTO CREDITS: © Eileen Hart: title page and page 13; © Renee Brady: pages 4, 5, 7, 9, 11, 15, 17, 19, 22; © Malcolm Romain: page 21.

Editor: Robert Stengard-Olliges

Cover design by Michelle Moore.

Library of Congress Cataloging-in-Publication Data

Thames, Susan.
  Our muscles / Susan Thames.
     p. cm. -- (Our bodies)
  Includes bibliographical references and index.
  ISBN 978-1-60044-512-5 (Hardcover)
  ISBN 978-1-60044-673-3 (Softcover)
  1. Muscles--Juvenile literature. I. Title.
  QP321.T43 2008
  612.7'4--dc22
                                        2007011809

Printed in the USA

CG/CG

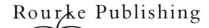

Rourke Publishing

www.rourkepublishing.com – rourke@rourkepublishing.com
Post Office Box 3328, Vero Beach, FL 32964

OUR MUSCLES

ROURKE DISCOVERY LIBRARY

Washington Elementary School
423 West Kincaide Street
Warsaw, IN 46580

Table of Contents

Muscles   4

Your Muscular System   12

Healthy Muscles   20

Glossary   23

Index   24

Muscles

Bend your arm.

Feel the **muscles** in your arm.

Muscles are under your skin.

You use your muscles to smile.

9

You use your muscles to **frown**.

11

Your Muscular System

Your body has over 600 muscles.

Your muscles move your body.

15

Some muscles work all the time.

Some muscles you choose
to use.

19

Healthy Muscles

Your muscles need eggs, cheese and meat.

21

Your muscles need **exercise**.

Glossary

exercise (EK sur size) — to move your body in a way that makes you strong and healthy

frown (FROUN) — a look on your face when you are sad or mad

muscles (MUHSS uhlz) — tissues that move different parts of your body

Index

arm   4, 5

exercise   22

move   14

skin   6

work   16

Further Reading

Lindeen, Carol. *My Muscles*. Pebble Books, 2007.

Powell, Jillian. *Moving*. Smart Apple Media, 2005.

Websites to Visit

www.kidshealth.org

www.healthfinder.gov/kids

www.yucky.discovery.com

About the Author

Susan Thames, a former elementary school teacher, lives in Tampa, Florida. She enjoys spending time with her grandsons and hopes to instill in them a love of reading and a passion for travel.